A hotel maid is visited by the Holy Spirit, an ex child star finds temporary solace in a baby-dreaded rent boy, and an assortment of drifters, wastrels and lost girls seek transcendence and good times in the alternate universe that is "Wayward". Part autobiographical exorcism, part analysis of the myth of the fallen woman, *Wayward* brings a haunting and unexpected perspective to being "on the road".

To Clay,

Autumn Border
Country talent Cobra

Love, Ah

Wayward
Ali Riley

Drawings by
Meghan Hildebrand

Frontenac House
Calgary, Alberta

Book design by EPIX Design Inc. Cover design by Ali Riley.
Cover image and drawings by Meghan Hildebrand

National Library of Canada Cataloguing in Publication Data

Riley, Ali.
 Wayward / Ali Riley.

Poems.
ISBN 0-9732380-3-8

I. Title.
PS8585.I53W39 2003   C811'.6   C2003-910019-7
PR9199.4.R542W39 2003

Frontenac House gratefully acknowledges the support of Canada Council for the Arts and The Alberta Foundation for the Arts for our publishing program.

Printed and bound in Canada.
Published by Frontenac House Ltd.
1138 Frontenac Avenue S.W.
Calgary, Alberta, T2T 1B6, Canada
Tel: 403-245-2491 Fax: 403-245-2380
editor@frontenachouse.com   www.frontenachouse.com

2nd Printing 2006

For my Mother

Acknowledgements

I am deeply indebted to Verna Relkoff, Almeda Glenn Miller and Tom Wayman of the KSA Writing Studio (now the Nelson Fine Arts Centre) for their help in editing the poems and stories that became Wayward.

Many thanks to Patricia Young for her kind encouragement.

"Sex Tangles" began as a musical performance piece. Thanks to Tim Campbell and Bartok Guitarsplat for their collaboration and inspiration. (Sacred Heart R.I.P.)

The Justine poems evolved out of the plays *Philosophy in the Bedroom* and *Hole in My Heart the Size of My Heart*. Parts of "Cold on the Shoulder" began as scenes in *dog dream*. I'd like to thank directors Jim Millan and Layne Coleman and all the cast members for their input into the original scripts.

Thanks also to: friends and family for their love and support, Nancy Jo Cullen, Joni Clarke, John Gould, Rose Cullis, Sheri-D Wilson, Daniel MacIvor, Nadia Ross, Stephen Seabrook, Michael Edwards, Blake Brooker, Christy Cameron (Dirty Babette), Michael Turner, the Single Onion folks, Meghan Hildebrand, Clay McCann & the Obliterati crew, Emma Greenstreet, Natasha Shannon, Irene Mock, Exene Cervenka and Fred Wah. Thanks always to Sanny and Sandy. Big love to Noam Ash.

And to K.C., who made it out alive.   Selah.

contents

Aspects of the Drift

Available Light

Lost Girls

Cold on the Shoulder

Aspects of the Drift

Aspects of the Drift

Hobo legend speaks of the drift. Hobo legend speaks of riding a boxcar and cares disappearing. All your earthly, daily concerns. Nothing exists but the cool night air and the stars. That, my friend, is the drift.

*

Flip-flops, front porches, fat possums. Playing the spoons in your underwear.

*

Backwards in a pickup truck – nothing but trees at a crazy angle.

*

Lying down in the middle of the highway. Standing up through a sun roof.

*

Small town grocery stores, the kind that sell live bait and have a slamming screen door. Playing kick-the-can after dark.

*

40's cotton dresses and galoshes. Ironing your clothes with a skillet.

*

Running away from home at 13 and staying at a hostel in Victoria with your best friend. You meet a crow-faced hippie and his friend. You're cold in the park so he gives you a poncho to wear, so now you're walking around town in this stupid poncho. He keeps trying to hold your hand. Can't he see you're a *seeker*? How can you gain insight into his angelic hobo soul when he's trying to cop a feel and he's already under your jean jacket?

*

Fire escapes. Discarded mattresses. No two alike.

*

Being stranded in a strange town, in a strange bar, watching an ethereal insect on the other side of the window. Transparent and fine, golden on the glass beneath the 2-for-1 steak sign. It looks like a fairy. Tapping at the window, aching for company, for the light. *Next lifetime, little one.*

*

Dancing in a sweatbox apartment, amiable and dirty.

*

Lying on the highway, just the two of you. No rides, middle of nowhere – mountain goats watching. The two of you on warm black asphalt. Sunny, late-winter day. Everything else gone, irrelevant. Your aliases, your stolen bluejeans. Nothing but the clothes on your backs and a pocket full of skunk weed, but you're not broke. You're on the drift.

*

Your first contact with the drift: approaching a treehouse in a new neighborhood. Uptight bully kid: "You can't come up here unless you're a member." Elizabeth hops from the tree: snaggle-toothed, Sun-Kist blonde hair, Malibu Barbie tan, orange and pink hotpants. Never seen her before. "Touch this card." You touch it. "You're a member!" She flings a piece of old cardboard over her shoulder. She's jumping barefoot in the dirt and hugging you.

*

In shark culture, one must keep moving. That is the law – from *Val de ree, Val de rah* happy-wanderer childhood to Kerouac adolescence.

*

Incidentally, Jack Kerouac almost got you killed.

*

Last day of summer, half a joint of shake, half a finger of Jack –
paradise for a hobo-girl. Flicking a fuschia Bic, sporting a red and
white kerchief, feet covered with scabs and bug-bites.

*

"Yeah. I'm on the drift. Whattaya expect."

Dream Home

White Trash Haiku #9
Gopher tails; bullets
A pocket of dangerous things
Makes a boy start fires

At the end of the cul-de-sac,
we built a fort in the weeds.
Children burnt brown,
covered with clay –
sitting cross-legged,
cool and ancient
amid the squealing tires
of teenage summer.

Rows and rows of dream homes
Paradise
where slaps and
places touched
were hidden in rooms
hidden in houses
hidden behind giant garages
rows and rows of perfect lawns.

Where we children ran
was nowhere like that
it was wild
wild roses, indian paintbrush,
stinkweed, silver sage,
long long grass.
Skeletons of two-by-fours
and drywall –

crushed slurpee cups, broken beer bottles
rusty wire, badger holes and
sticks with colored plastic ribbon telling us
this refuge would not last.

Another row of dream homes
floor plans repeated
in intervals of five
all down the block.

Rows and rows,
like the songs of dead soldiers
and poppies we learned in school
we are the dead
loved and were loved
and now we lie in Flanders Field.

In the fort we built
the girls smelled like weeds
The boys were nailing kittens to trees.

Later the boys play chicken
with lit cigarettes and knives.
The girls already expert
at dissecting themselves.

Sugar Coma

All Hallows
the membrane between this world and the next
is starting to tear

They hunker now
in the marigolds
the hoarfrost
the folds
of a torn white sheet
the Silent Ones
walk among us
the witching hour
when midnight becomes light
becomes chaos

Halloween night
Kiddy-speech howls
with beings unseen,
spinning cataract webs
behind trick or treat eyes
spinning from beyond the veil
a torn white sheet
a long slow keen –

It's almost time for the membrane to tear

This is the witching hour
When night becomes chaos
becomes light
fritzing and frazzling
till
pop.

The Silent Ones are coming through
Cherry pop mouth
poking through cloth
Sugar Coma eyes
Cheeks blazing with lipstick
(*Cherries in the Snow*)

it's time for the membrane to tear

up and down the street
crazy from candy
sucker-red lips
stick through
a hole
in a white sheet
blurt out dead dialects

out of the mouths of babes
spill savage, joyful,
long-forgotten words

Singing sad in
languages lost –
Hittite
Feliskan
Phoenician

the gift of glossolalia
comes so trippingly to the tongue
poking through

the hole
in the sheet.

Boo. *Boo.*

Two girls dressed as gypsies – breathless –
bright spots of rouge
chicken bone necklace
the Silent Ones come
bright spirits poke through
little girl eyes
their little girl mouths
now ancient and soaring with song

The Silent Ones
whisper
we are here
come with us
the children follow –

the ghost
of a scent
trails
down
the garden path
until it's neither
garden
nor path
nothing
but tangle of trees
patches of weeds

here

Silent Ones
take
their leave

Hotel Fire

White Trash Haiku # 66: The National Hotel
Inside the radiator
a heater-man sharpening his long knife –
Scrape. Scrape. *Squeeeeeee.*

What makes a man start fires?

She died burning, her arms around another married man.
Unloved, inhaling the smoke.
Someone adored her once
he spoke of her like a saint
a tarnished angel.
A lost girl who came to him fully and without guile,
bringing glamour to his lunch break
in this tiny town.
The wildest thing he'd known.
A wild thing, a stray, from outside.
She'd wait for him in a motel village –
flipping magazines, listening to the radio
to the radiator
to the sound of an empty room.

He'd come with sandwiches and coffee
Soon it would be time to cast the magazine aside
Soon it would be time to reapply lipstick
(*Cherries in the Snow*)
To return to perfume counter/luncheonette/reception desk
she was careful of marking him –
"I'll wash it off" he'd laugh
and crush her
mouth to his
"You always look like a bad girl after I kiss you"
he'd say.

"*You* always look like a clown."

She had to leave
She was bigger than that town
bigger than life.
Go West, young girl
Walking, walking with no purpose
she caught the eye of strangers and held it.
Often touched by them,
she was brave.
Brave, but so lost.
If only I could be there
I could find her
I could tap her shoulder as she
walks her somnambulant walk
I could stop what has to happen.

Take Hold of Yourself

White Trash Haiku # 21: Green River Killer
She is in his comfort zone.
The door locks automatically.
This is it. *Here we go.*

Cold on the shoulder
outside the town
she's been waiting too long
around the corner
slides another car
and another
a 70's mid-size
squeaking the corn snow

A Jim Rockford car
a few payments past due
inside, a traveling salesman
on a losing streak.
Despair hangs in the weave
of a tweed jacket
never sent to the cleaners
flop sweat
leather coat
Player's Lights
Florsheims un-shined.

*Pedal to the metal and we're
only passing through
this baby's falling hard
hard for you*

the heater and the music on
matchbook/8-track
Muskrat Love

take hold of yourself we are riding

Outside the town
inside the warm car,
the haystacks are flipping past.
They look like loaves of bread. Manna from Heaven.
She's got her head rolled over the back of the seat
St. Teresa receiving her ecstasy.
Raising her eyes skyward.

take hold of yourself we are riding

She's somewhere else
lying in the back seat of Daddy's Torino
carried from Sunday dinner
warm, blanket-wrapped
a streetlight's beam
catches the hood of the car
hands it off to the next beam
and the next
pushed by friendly lights
to a safe home

take hold of yourself we are riding

She's got her eyes rolled back,
she's 'luded, stolen.
She dreams of velvet.

> *Of butterfly heartbeats,*
> *their silk staccato*
> *staccato*
> *staccato*
> *silk staccato*
> *now a violent*
> *violent*
> *hum.*

She dreams of velvet.

She conjures the arc of a walnut tree

deep in the forbidden city.
Under it the lion uncurls and slouches
to the other side
of the city wall.
He's hunting miracles and little girls.
What better place than outside the gates.
Past the desert,
the farmlands
she's speeding
through.

take hold of yourself we are riding

On a lone autumn afternoon
the lone gunman
loads a lonely bullet
into his lonely gun.

take hold of yourself we are riding

"Kiss...
...this guy"
she sighs
and
rolls her face on the
cool foggy glass
of the passenger window.

Ghost Daughter

You can't talk to your daughter
she rolls her eyes
she looks daggers
screams "Hypocrite!"
screams "Stolen Land!"

Her scars are a drug
nothing stops the blood
in her head
like letting it
flow

across to show
down to go

ladders up her arms
her legs
ladders to her head
ladders to her heart
her wrists
her ankles
down her right thigh
a graceful
not-quite-healed
snake

she's traded her birthright
for a beat she can dance to
dark corner
crimson tide
X carved through a new pair of tights

she fondles a matchbook
if she were a boy
she might try arson
or bar fights
but she is a girl
so she takes it out
on the nearest
available
bit of flesh.

A delicate operation –
opening yourself
to pins and needles,
the harsh white light
of a small porcelain room

"She's indestructible" they say
"She couldn't destroy herself
even if she tried"
and try she does
fitting and gnashing
sexing the chaos.

You thought you saw her
creeping into the master bedroom
knife between her teeth –
leading an army of
vengeful children.

The nation's bathrooms are full
adolescents acting out
a dimly remembered
ascetic past –
they are possessed
overcome

their bodies host old souls
an angry tribe
centuries dead
they are fasting
seeing visions
bloodletting

a sleeping shaman lies
in your bathtub
as you floss your teeth
he opens one eye
whispers
"we shall live again"

You can't talk to your daughter
she runs the gauntlet
from back door to bedroom
she shoots through the family room
like an arrow
wearing that jacket you despise
a ghost shirt
deflecting your gaze, your questions
Her door slams upstairs
her music begins
artillery bass
bass
bass
now her footsteps
are dancing
dancing
like a warrior.

Available Light

Five More Positions of a Retired Child Star

Position Number 1.
Your head
shot has been bounced
around town
like a child of divorce
you try not to feel desperate
though no reasonable offer is refused
be it game show
or infomercial –

you remember when the series still ran the day you were shooting
at Griffith observatory and girl scouts screamed your name
while you stood on the winding staircase out of eye and ear shot
mincing and mimicking for the benefit of a bored PA (whose job
was keeping them away) and later that day you overheard
wardrobe ask your tutor "What do you two even *talk* about?" and
your tutor sneered "Oh you know. Stuff he wants to buy." So still
later when your tutor gives you a hug you smile until your head
passes her shoulder. Your ten year old face sets – immaculate.
Blank.

You ate an Oreo and watched them light your stand-in and then
the old gaffer brought in a light to "give you some sparkle". "It's
an Obie" he said, "Merle Oberon's husband invented it to light
up her eyes" and smiled kindly at you.

– you've been floating forever
in the zircon lounge
dawn finds you fishing
for compliments
fetching
for fools
frisky as a convict
in May.

Position Number 2.
How sweet it is
to finally fall
from child star
to talent cobra
to have nothing
to do with afternoons
but troll
for jailbait
down Sunset

sleep tight
NAMBLA Rambla
may your limp life
explode
in tinsel
trust fund
trash

Position Number 3.
this town is chock-full of chicken hawks
and Special Ones
who got off the bus pretty
these fascinators
the most likely
their skid-towns ever saw.

It ain't enough.
But the magic hour still comes
every day.

Position Number 4.
I would drink
till I was full
and then I would feel
empty
and then I would drink
again.

Position Number 5.
You spy a blonde skate kid. Silky baby-dreads, stepped-on angel
face. He stretches, his too-washed t-shirt riding up to expose a
sliver of belly, a waxing moon of skin-show. Luminous, golden.
You stop the car. He gets in. You reach to touch that impossible
stomach as you drive with one hand down Sunset Blvd.

Kiddy flesh.

Subcutanous fat adds to the delectability. They say Marilyn's skin
was soft like that. You take him home and feed him poptarts,
koolaid and vodka. He tells you he had a crush on you in Grade
2. In reruns. He says he's thinking about seratonin boosters, what
do you think? You reach for his belt buckle and say the one thing
about Prozac is it tends to make people rearrange their shelves
too much. While he's bent over the patio table he picks up your
cell and dials. "Guess who's fucking me right now!" You reach for
a bottle of Locker Room and pump harder. The kid is saying "I
can't believe you don't know that show! You know, he's that
guy!" You grab the phone and throw it into the pool.

take what you're given you say
as you shoot
in available light.

You Folded

White Trash Haiku #38
An infinite heart –
fortunate to own, if a saint.
If a sinner, less so.

You folded into me on our friend's fucked-out couch. The sight of
the top of your head, graying temple (still vigorous), your porno-
glaze. I gazed at you, attached to me, smothered in softness,
aggression quelled. Old alpha-male, top gorilla.
The man one sees at a gala in a monkey suit. I pictured a secret
bag of tricks, a place of surrender buried in black cloth. A
renegade priest.

What is it about making a man forget his vows?
It's not difficult, they're as easy to smash as crockery. Men and
mountains can be moved through various vile peccadilloes. My
specialty – sexual alchemy. Turning indifference into gold. The
room gets smaller, the air more concentrated –
like morning urine. Much too strong. For words. For rules.

We're on another plane. A high one. Utterly myopic. Within this
square I spent you – the place where no movement is possible.
Sticky, trapped legs filled with honey. Stuck.

I keep thinking I'll never live through this but I do. Over and
over, the little deaths finally adding up to one complete one. I
crave immobility to the point I cast *myself* down, free as an
unhitched trailer on an 8% grade. I take a flying leap into the
void and miss, then hobble my way through deceitful
concubine-hood.

I am Icarus, but it is downwards I seek, burning my broken wings with the smoke of Hell.

Hell, I could do better, but do I want to? Why not wallow awhile with my pig-people. Snuffling and snorting lines off a table made of linoleum wood. Nodding off in front of the jukebox.
You can't sleep in here. You can't sleep in here.

Joy

The baby Jesus has been messing
with this year's festivities.

He's tampered with the toys –
Nintendo game cubes have been melting
down mid-battle
"get some sunshine" the screen suddenly flashes
"hug your Mom."

An over-accessorized Diva-Doll's pulled string
causes her to purr, whiskey-voiced,
anti-Celine
"there's no reason at all to buy into this shit, ya know."

Baby Jesus has been sitting in
as Santa, tells a kid –
"Some people don't know how to love. They're damaged. Don't
take it personally."

Yesterday He caused all the computerized signs
in the Western world
to flash "GLUT! GLUT! GLUT!" at 20 minute intervals.

He sits at the throne of Wonderland
in a low-rent mall
surrounded by despondent, minimum-wage elves.
He beams at them over his flammable beard and they become
infused, enthused
smile for the first time in weeks.

A tired teen hustles by with her crying child.
"We're late!" she hisses, clutching an elbow as the little girl's
head swivels, exorcist style, towards the giant candy canes and
cotton batten snow.

Nooooo Mommmmm!
The mother ignores the screams of *Santaaaaa!*
and the litany of

I want!
I want!
I want!

The mother floats in a miasma of Christmases past.
Her early ones with the no-gift fake-out
"I guess Santa forgot you."
the brave face put on for as long as the joke stayed funny, the
rush of emotion when the gift was finally
trotted into the living room –

her last Christmas at home – her fourteenth –
when she came home late on Christmas Eve.
She sits topless on the family room couch
her arms crossed
(she still has her baby fat)
her tank top ripped
by her father
She cries while she's being questioned
Where were you at 6
at 7

at 8 o clock?
The interrogation continues
with studded belt and hair dryer
The angel on the tree keeps quiet
No silvery voice sings
Peace on earth

As she drags the shrieking 2-year-old into the parking lot her
skirt may as well still be flipped up
the residue of a beating may as well still draw blood.

She was so beautiful when she danced in Black Light
at the teen centre.
They called her *Tequila Girl*.

In the parking lot she grits her teeth, throws the kid in the child
seat and starts the car.
Her baby stops crying. She holds a treat, bought from the loonie-
a-throw bubblegum toy machine at Wal-Mart, a shut-the-fuck-up
consolation prize for the anguish of walking dozens of aisles of
floor-to-ceiling unattainables.

The child opens the plastic blob of welfare trash and finds the
trinket inside.
A troll doll of some sort. A disappointment.
Then – PuLL! – it folds out tall
the length of a Barbie, a face of ineffable kindness replacing the
usual zombo-stare
with another twist it further transforms –
not from Japanese robot to intergalactic destroyer-god
no! Triple-hinged Wings, finer than sparrow –
emerge from iridescent shoulder blades
a flawed and splendid angel hovers
fills the Subaru with light
tells Mother and daughter
You are Loved.

"If You Think They Don't Go Crazy In Tiny Rooms"

He left a star-shaped stain in the middle of the Motel 6 floor.
So much for *that* party trick, she thinks.
She came in here eight days ago to vacuum,
now she languishes like Catherine Deneuve in *Repulsion*.
He's taken to hiding
piles of powder for her to find,
powder she's afraid to try.
Would it rev her up or slow her down?
Where is he anyway?
Has it really been over a week?
Her beige maid's dress, not quite a colour,
more like all flavours of boredom
melted into one sad shade.
Not a pinch of interest to this outfit,
but for the tiny speck of chipped nail polish
(*Scarlet Pimpernel*)
nestled in the waffle-weave.

These are deluxe accommodations,
but she's still not sure why she's here.
She received a stack of tens on the bedside table two days ago
but since then nothing but the star.
This stain.

"Stella" she says out loud, looking at it.
The air conditioner sighs along with her,
feel, see, whisper, listen, it says.
soar however you can, extols the bar fridge
its pitch rising,
it adopts a wheedling tone –
soar you must!
with brandy, with words, with graceful appetite –
she finally unplugs it.
she finds a plastic sign hanging from the doorknob.
"Maid – please make this room sing with your spirit"
and on the other side, simply
"Please be profound".

This melanine and Fortrel won't yet help her transcend,
but they ache to be used
to climb to heaven.
All things, even the pock-marked
mystery-stained upholstery
of a motel chair
(especially that!)
beg to be used for something other than
dull, vile practices.

Direct your attention to this burn
on the couch. See where the fabric
melts into beads?
This is where the Voice will speak
two days from now.

In her wilder days
she thoughtlessly rolled
joints in the parchment
of Gideon's Bible.
Leaves of Grass!
In the words of G-d!
Suddenly this horrifies her.

What Emissary will speak to her
in this place
anonymous as an airport
neither here nor there?

She will be suddenly silent.
She will mute the Nashville Network
and stare down the grate in the wall.
She will wail,
she will discover her purpose
on this neutral ground.

She will put her head down
she will hear the rustle
hear it settle
she will feel herself to be alone
then she will
be.

Footnote to Footnote to Footnote to Howl: Holy!

Holy Holy Holy
The world is holy! The soul is holy! The skin is holy! The nose is holy!
The tongue and cock and hand and asshole holy! Everything is holy
everybody holy every boy an angel – holy the madman – holy!
– Allen Ginsberg

Holy the baby-mama. Ankles angled behind her neck. In the
passenger seat of a Trans Am Freedom Eagle. Pregnant before her
feet hit the floor. Holy!

Holy the chicken hawk. Silent sobbing into the Triple 5 Soul
sweat shirt back of a rent boy. Holy!

Holy the feline-faced got-a-secret girl. Low slung pants, high, fly
chest – a fox among wolves, she is rufied. Chocolate drunk,
steam-cleaned, she slides to the floor with a velvety ploomf.
Holy!

Holy slut-born, slut-to-the-end.
Doxie. Tramp. Chippie. Cougar.
They laugh at your out-of-date ass. Your second suitor of the day
offers you Band-Aids and cola for your whiskey. You thank him
from the bottom of your corned and calloused heart. Holy!

Holy the ninja farmers. Holy the trustafarians. Unshaved,
unwashed tribal girls.
You scare jailbait and CEO alike. Your anti-social refusal to trim
is tantamount to treason to the airstrip dogma of our times. This
thicket of thatch – hey
It's a jungle down there – holy!

Holy the lost girl. Wet lips hover over snakeskin. Booze can, beyond Metallica, her armour is suddenly misplaced. Her shell becomes soft. (You could swallow her whole.)
She drops the tough talk, a timid walk home – holy.

Holy the anorexic. Putting herself under. Counting back from 10. Size 8, size 4, size 0. Holy!

Sorrow can't be sorrow all the time. Neither can joy. Holy.

Holy bad choice bitch. When buddy pulls his dick out to change position she spies a big glob of girl-come stuck on a gnarly vein. Solid evidence of her foolhardiness, President's Choice could bottle it; call it *Memories of No Boundaries.*
"Holy S---," she whispers. "What am I doing here?"

Holy the guttersnipe gender outlaw. (Every boy's an angel). Glucose fructose fuck-toy making mama moan all night. Hot cherry Popsicle mouth. Every boy's an angel. You look so pretty in my 50-cent dress – holy. You take it strong from a 9" glitter-cock – holy. You make it sing

(*rock star rock star rock star rock star*)

Holy!

Our bodies are holy. What we've put them through – holy. The pull-a-train endless dawn-drags – holy. The solitude of stun – holy. The daily grind, the trouble nights – holy.

I can still taste disgrace
onions and ether
in the back of my throat
seven year shame-cycle
anaesthesia sits in the liver
till the cells turn over

SHOUT IT OUT – HOLY!

Shout you unclean nubile! Holy!
Shout out your layer of rot. Holy!
Detritus of summer's past. Holy.
Shout what's left to burn. Holy.

and vanish, holy.
and disappear – holy.
not petroleum by-product melting into a bead
silk shrivel to ash
holy

Lost Girls

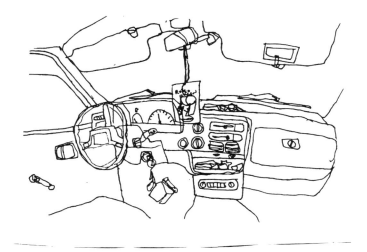

"*… a child is missing…*"
-a voice through a megaphone from a slow-passing car
(startled out of sleep, Parkdale, July 1991)

Dark Sparkle: c 1975 Her true name, a farm-girl derivative of Lorelei, the spirit/sprite that appears in dark waters, luring men to death by drowning. Hitchhiker. Patti Smith fan. Like all lost girls, an "immortal daemon among the wholesome children."

Hottentot Venus: 1779-1815 A Koisan from Capetown known as "Saartjie", Sara Baartman was lured to England by British Marine Sergeant William Dunlop. He saw a future in her body, and told her European aristocracy would pay to look at her protruding buttocks (medical term: steatopygia). She dies alone 5 years later and is preserved in formaldyhyde by Georges Cuvier, Napoleon's surgeon.

Clementine: c 1864 Dressed in calico, stalking the fields. Abundance, quintillions. Reminiscent of *Christina's World. Man with a Hoe.*

Lolita: c 1948 Eternal archetype.

The Black Dahlia: 1924-1947. Black hair. Red lips. White body cut in two.

Justine: Published 1791 by Aphonse Donatien Francois Sade. Taken as pseudonym by Mary Crews, 1975.

Inger: c 1888 Hans Christian Andersen: The girl who trod on a loaf. A peasant girl with a tendency towards cruelty (pulling the wings from flies), she is "given to some fine people". Whilst on her way to visit her poor parents she steps on a loaf of bread (to avoid soiling her new shoes) and sinks to Marshland.

Dark Sparkle

Dark Sparkle Speaks of Her Butterfly Past While traveling West, 1976

Brown sedan, Radium to Golden: A butterfly in a jar

Five years old, five doors down.
She skip-skitters (mother at work
father mowing the lawn)
empty Miracle
Whip jar
the butterfly is caught

hoary elfin

the back gate explodes
the father's hand emerges
wrapped in a towel
blue roses consumed by thirsty red
two fingers gone (lawn mower)

her fault

the week before she'd faked suicide

with steak knife and cochineal

made for valentines

"I've never been suicidal, though. I faked it once when I was five.
Oh, my family went on a picnic or something. I was real upset.
So I dragged a chair over to the baking shelf and got the red food
colouring. Cochineal it's called. Oh, remember those silver ball
bearings that used to be on cupcakes? They were scary. Anyway I
got the red and sprinkled it all over, in the general direction of
my heart, you know, like I've stabbed myself. I just lay there all
twisted on the floor till I got bored and cleaned it all up and hid
in the garage. No wonder I got into gore films."

a lifelong taste for mayhem
drawn away from nursery morality
to the unexpurgated gore
Cinderella's stepsister's amputated toes

the biting teeth of the big bad wolf

Blue pick-up truck, Golden to Sicamous: Butterflies and Minks

(I tell you this because I want you to like me.
I don't want to die in a ditch.)
"The oldest boyfriend I'd had up to that point was Steven.
Brilliant, 21, totally nuts. He spoke a pidgin Bavarian he made up
himself. Told me I had the softest stomach he'd ever seen. He
wasn't really mine. Justine gave him to me one night at her
Mom's. We were all smoking Lebanese Blonde, and she whispers
to me, 'He's yours now. Just wait until you see how good he is.'
So he carried me downstairs. 'Break it Up' was playing. Patti
Smith. After that I had to share him with Justine, some girl from
Willow Park and Darla Gold. He had two classifications of girls -
butterflies and minks. I was a mink. Darla Gold was a mink too.
Sexy, sultry Darla Gold, who chain-smoked Virginia Slims.
Blonde with a black-hole soul. *Nothing* California about her at
all, she was Suzanne Somers by way of Samuel Beckett. We were
the only two minks in the neighbourhood, all the other girls were
butterflies, according to him. Darla's younger sister, Debbi, the
perky one. My friend Fawn. They wore white pants with pink
panties showing through. They had key chains shaped like
adorable cartoon characters. They drew unicorns. Their clothes
were cute, the colour of breakfast cereal. Gigglers. Darla never
giggled. I don't think I ever saw her crack a smile. Every time I
saw her pissed-off face, I was thrilled and horrified to be included
in her company. A real woman."

Gold LTD, Sicamous to Chase: Floats Like a Butterfly

(She shared a name with a prizefighter, perhaps the greatest of all
time. It means: *exalted one*.)
On the morning of the Thrilla in Manilla she painted her
fingernails blue (*Cutex: sea anemone*)
and practiced giving the finger to the mirror.
See – she's not a sucky little fem anymore.
Quiet girls get picked on. Wild girls write their own ticket.

"I remember when I first started getting noticed by guys. It all
happened so fast. One night Randy Warshawsky tried to fuck me
at Shannon Grant's babysitting job. We were drunk on shit mix
and he tried to stick it in while 'Longfellow Serenade' by Neil
Diamond played out in the living room. He couldn't manage it
('something in the way,' he said) and the next morning he
spreads all over school that I'm deformed. That there's 'some kind
of skin growing there'. I'm like, the last virgin in the 8th grade.
All day long all the boys, even the goobers that don't even hang
out with Randy and those guys, keep bugging me, chanting my
name, sarcastically – 'Ali! Boom ba yay!'"

The sucky little fem is scared, but the prizefighter in her says
 "Hey," hands spread, "Here I am. Here I fucking am."

Lost Girl Satellites

Around these seven girls spin satellites. Riding, circulating.
Sniffing like dogs. Some good, some bad.
Protector/predator, who can tell? We've all been wrong before.

John the Revelator: Lost Girl Satellite #1

Born: 1943, John Marshall
Convicted 1985 for the murders of 12 young women.

the demon is my Siamese twin
kill it and you kill me.
we share too many organs.

I'm not afraid to die

Hottentot Venus

Little Girls Love Pink
Red for blood
white for purity
colour of duality
secret shivers, wrecked lives
filched paperbacks
thumbed
for filthy parts
the colour of *Candy*

fluffy dress
valentine
icing

our walls   mouth
our beds   pussy
pink defines us   asshole

Saartjie's remains are being returned to Africa. There will be singing. The ancestors watch.

Lured by promises, Sara Baartman was not so different from our girls. We are all sisters under the mink. Consider her captor, his smooth words. Lost girls are suckers for pimp-talk. And he needed to have a whole continent to name his darkness after.
gold
sugar
spice
coca
poppy
Her remains are being returned. Her bones, her heart, her vulva, preserved in formaldhyde,

a butterfly in a jar.

Clementine

On the Prairies
Some get lost in the blizzard on the way to the barn and aren't found until spring, if ever. You have to tie a rope to hold to keep you safe. Once you're lost you're lost and the footsteps you take to find your way only remove you further from home.

Earth, Air
The good townspeople choose Earth as their final place to rest. The good townspeople are merchants, bankers. The elementals of earth are Gnomes – keepers of gold. A banker's hands are as smooth as a fancy-woman's. It is feminine to be buried. The arms of mother earth.

Open burial is for outlaws. (Also practiced by certain Plains tribes.) The outlaws lie in open air, where they fell, to be consumed by air and the beasts of the land. The birds of the field. The elementals of air are Sylphs – keepers of adventure. To be consumed where you land is a masculine death. Billy the Kid picked clean on the mesa.

Fire
I think it is brave to die by fire. It does not seem that such a death would go unwitnessed. It is spectacle. Fit for martyrs and fanatics. The elementals of fire are Salamanders – keepers of courage. Joan of Arc and Varanasi widows. Witches. It is a masculine death but often reserved for those women who threaten the male status quo.

Water
A watery death is achingly female. A girl with a heart broken by sorrow or madness. A watery death is a solitary death. Ophelia. Darling Clementine. The elementals of water are Ondines keepers of sorrow and joy. It's a feminine death, as feminine as sky burial is masculine. Into the arms of the river you go. Female death draws you under – under the ground. Under the water. Male death reaches for the sky. The flames. The ether.

Clementine

> *Oh my darling*
> *Oh my darling*
> *Oh my darling Clementine*
> *You are lost and gone forever*
> *Dreadful sorry, Clementine*

The song talks about Clementine's delicate feet. Like an angel, a fairy she walked. Lightly, so lightly. Trip the light fantastic. She was made for finery, flowers. A hope chest filled with dainties. She keeps house for her father, the miner. Her mother, Thora, died in childbirth. In the middle of a snow storm.

Wetigo got the miner and he got her. The song talks about her delicate feet. When the spirit left him he'd cradle her feet to his chest like a baby, the only part of her unsullied. To him her feet were *she* when she was days old and her Mother lay out in the snow. His rage was such that day that he threw Clementine out after her, where she lay screaming until he changed his mind and fetched her.

Dreadful sorry, Clementine.

The song tells how she tripped and fell.
Face down on the ground there's nowhere else to fall.
Wetigo got him.
And he got her.
Dreadful sorry, Clementine.

Water to drink

Clementine. Her feet were so pretty. Itty bitty baby feet. Cradled and cried over. *"Your itty bitty sooties,"* the miner would croon.

Clementine received a diary for her ninth birthday, pretty as a hymnal, covered with sky blue kid. She wrote in it every day.

I like to sit by the river. So easily, so quickly could it all be over. Someone behind you, a push a shove, – into the water and carried away. It's easy to get carried away beside a river. The river sees all, takes all.

On sunny days she always likes to be by the river. She becomes the sprightly daughter, the darling girl skipping so trippingly from rock to rock. Her father watches her and smiles. She swivels around, feet perched. A shaky wave. She rights herself. Smiles. Turns again to the river.

Drown and you drown alone. Burn and the town comes running.

'Twas a Miner, 49-er
He watches from the bank, the spirit no longer inside.
Able to feel proud, happy. Light, even. "My *darling Clementine*" he thinks.
He looks at their cabin.
He sees her mother, Thora, standing in the doorway, heavy with her.
How could there have been be so much snow.

(he lights the torch)

The Miner Sings of Thora as the Cabin Burns

I promised Thora, when we wed
Baby's breath and fountains
Now the hours fall like lead
It's whiskey, death and mountains

The river's dark and frozen now
It's 39 below
In the deadest deadwood winter
days will pass molasses slow

I came from a land of roses
The flowers I'll not again know
my life for a pocket of posies
Sunk deep in a river of snow

Once upon a sunny day
'twas baby's breath and fountains
Dreadful sorry, Girl, to say
It's whiskey, death and mountains

Yonder lies my baby mine
Still yonder lies my lover
My baby's breath blows crystalline
Beneath her soft white cover

The day we wed I said there'd be
Baby's breath and fountains
The only thing that's left for me
Is whiskey, death and mountains

I came from a land of roses
Back I shall never go
I came from a land of roses
But dreamed of a land of snow

John the Revelator

something has been unleashed.
It is unleashed and out in the world.
It has found its feet.
It will splatter the walls in the house of heaven.

The (bloody) red
cactus fruit
(her heart)
being offered to the sun.
full dress ceremony

coca leaves
adulation

is this not what all lost girls seek?
A dramatic, poignant death.

iron bells
1789

[contact]

Justine

Find a patch of weeds
Bury my body without ceremony
Erect no monument
– Last Will and Testament, *Alphonse Donatien François Sade*

The pupil surpasses the teacher

Mary Crews chooses the name Justine. The innocence of the
Justine character in the face of all debauchery appeals to her. She
knows in her bones there's nothing stable for her to emulate.
"Matter is not static. It's up to us to mimic it or die. We are
Bowie's Young Americans," she says. "We are shape shifters.
Nowhere is somewhere for us. We like the world best when its
going 70 mph past our window."

Mall-rat libertines. Sade would be proud of these children with
claws. The fort-magic of childhood holds in adolescence with
liquor, drugs and intrigue. Chocolate mesc. Crystal meth. The
battles can be bloody, we fight with namchuks and other,
nameless martial devices, with California our Magic Kingdom:
shiny cathedral to our vague longings.

So we rejected everything we were given, Justine and I.
Derangement of the senses meant everything to us. We forged a
religion out of carnival rides and zodiac blotter. I knew her to be
truly valiant. She always had more guts than I did. A *Spiritus
Sanctus* slipping in and out of trouble, slithering – a serpent
weaving through my ribs into my cold, cold, heart.

*An exultation of larks from the mouth of the prettiest punk in
Hollywood.*

Dark Sparkle recalls Justine, 1983

> *And you – O desolate one. What does it mean that you dress*
> *in scarlet…That you enlarge your eyes with paint? Your lovers*
> *despise you – They seek your life*
> > *– Jeremiah 4: 30.*

She called herself Justine, after the book by the Marquis de Sade.
You know, he's like the guy who invented being a sadist? And she
loved the Dahlia. Dyed her hair Clairol blue-black, crow black,
just like hers. I measured my self against her. In her I saw the
beauty of distress.

We invented ourselves. We looked for clues to things we couldn't
decipher through our experiments.

> *you have to open the body to determine its meaning*

Neighbour boys, bobby pins

> *I want the red under your skin*
> *I want your skin under my nails*

Does it hurt when I do this?
I want to see how much you can take.
Spread your legs. Let me see you.

Justine as Snow White, 1975

Boyfriends? Boyfriends, no. I don't have boyfriends. I have
associates. Accomplices. We plot my destruction together.

I lost my mother's gold earring at a gang-bang in Forest Lawn.
This is what I had on: Cork-Eaze platforms, denim gauchos from
Junior Bazaar, a taupe French-cut t-shirt, a leopard chiffon scarf.

A keg party in someone's parents' unfinished basement. Spilled beer running down the floor drain. Grey army blankets tacked up, not quite touching the floor, make a room in the corner. A twin bed – no sheets one blanket. The usual posters. I went and lay down.

When I opened my eyes there was someone getting me. I was too tired to care. I just closed my eyes and thought of nothing. Another guy and I think one or two more. One of them said, "You know, it's weird. I can't get a hard-on. Is that bad?"

At one point my best friend barged in with a guy, looking for me. She told me later, "And I was with this cute guy, and I said you've got to meet my friend, and we pull back the blanket and there you are, just lying there naked. You looked really good, actually. Like Snow White."

John The Revelator

The light bulb in my head is so hot it would singe and frizzle the hair of any rodent.

They walk the street like puppets. You can see the wires flapping their jaw.

My wire is hot. Made of steel. Steel trap.

You, repentant whore.
You're trapped like a rat with steel-trap man.

Children Together Form a Beast

Slut – I always laughed at the word
Yelled from neighbour lawns.

> *take my jelly home and jam on it*

so I'm a slut so what

> *All hail those in whose eyes the title whore is an honour.*
> – Sade

I was feeling pretty dizzy, I wanted to lie down
So I went behind the sheet that was hung in the corner of the
basement
I guess it was someone's room.
It felt nice and cool, kinda hazy
I woke up in the dark
Surrounded by guys
I pretended to be asleep
And like all of a sudden there was all these guys all over me
They were bigger than just a couple of guys, this was like one big
heavy unit...

Your flesh is all mine
No longer prostrate
I swallow your charm
and spit out your hate

John the Revelator

This might seem awkward or strange right now but the ice will
melt very soon. There will be things we will share. Right now,
underneath the ground, things are starting to shift. The tectonic
plates are colliding like demon lovers. The lava's starting to flow.
This will cause the oceans to rise up and destroy the cities. Gone.
We haven't got a name for what will occur.
The world needs a gardener. A brutal one. And that's me.
Showering arsenic on the lawn.

The Black Dahlia

> *The beasts are against her...*
> *Come, ye birds of the field. Come to devour.*
>   – Jeremiah 12: 9.

"The Dahlia," Justine says, "I can see her turning on the radio and dancing in place as she does her eyeliner, then rouge. Lipstick always comes last. Then she puts on her good coat. She doesn't know it's her last night on earth."

First night in L.A., riding down Sunset, dragging the dawn too far. Back of a convertible. Heads backwards, topless, upside-down. *Flipping out* over the palm trees. Their boughs pass over us like fluffy false eyelashes.

Past the vacant lot where they found the Black Dahlia. Justine sits up and says, "Did you know they used to call her Snow White?"

> *So long little girl. You've burned your infinity.*

Untamed World
Nature is where they dump the bodies.

On the shoulder of the road (where there's nothing to buy) lies a patch of weeds. This tiny space, a stone's throw from the temples of commerce and speculation. The Vacant Lot. The end of the cul-de-sac where the weeds begin. The place no sane adult goes. Dogs, children and madmen.

The adults wait on the sidewalk while their dogs investigate this untamed world.

Los Angeles, January 15, 1947
If real estate is civilization then the vacant lot is nature.

"I am nature's faithful hound." – Humbert Humbert

A man arrives home from the graveyard shift. He's annoyed – the dog's chewed up the furniture again. He gets ready for bed, then thinks, better take him out. He throws his coat over his pyjamas and walks his dog to the end of the cul-de-sac. The dog bolts ahead. The man yawns. "What's that damn dog gotten into now?"

The flash goes off. There is a circle of yellow tape describing a small contained space. Inside the circle is a woman. Outside the circle are men. The man with the dog stands off to the side. More photos are taken. There is only one woman present and the men are careful about what they say.

The flash of a camera is cruel, sexy.

There's the unmistakable excitement of something awful about to happen. Of something awful that *has* happened. Everyone standing outside the circle is completely in the moment. No one is thinking of what they had for dinner. Some may be thinking of wives or daughters. One is reminded of a picture he saw in a magazine. At this particular second in this particular place no one is thinking a banal thought.

It was her last night
There was no moon. Black on black.
he pushed me ahead in the weeds
the tall grass was dark, so dark
against the sky
I could hear thousands of insects
creatures
it's so alive out here

Lolita

Nebraska
they travel through farmlands –

trail of tears

she the sullen pasture
on which he spills
his seed
Cherokee Nation chock-full of land-fill

they travel through desert –
weapons
lying spent in the sand
Los Alamos wafts with muzak.

missiles, arrows

The flash makes daylight brighter than ever.
"Let's move to Alaska" she says
as the bottom drops out of the grease pot
"It will be clean there"

the dripping leaves of the redwoods
blood must spill.

they ride through green, through mountains –
across the great divide the spirits are restless
with a painted hand to feed
and a slightly undernourished
vacuum-packed silence.

Lo-girl is riding. Lost to the world.
She kisses the driver –
barely brushing his cheek
a drive-by kiss
faint pink smear from mouth to bone
(*Cherries in the Snow*)

Oregon
They tear a joyride strip through
the honest labour
of saw mills and steel towns
passing
loggers, truckers –
diners, where Lo consumes
an unadorned hamburger on a misty day.
Thick plates, impossible to break.

Nights are made of winces and individually wrapped soaps
mornings are off to a late start
Passing the hitchhikers, two boys this time

Lolita:
"He got up very early. He was much too animated, flushed. When
we got to the door to leave he turned around right away and sat
down. Kicked off his shoes. Be it ever so Hum-ful there's no place
that's home. When he gets lusty his whole face changes – it gets
Germanic. Piggy-puddly. That wrinkle in his forehead, that
schitzoid scribble. Porno-glaze. He starts to purr and I know I'm
done for. Lately my trick has been to pretty much ignore him. He
got way more passionate, almost lost his head it seemed like.

Later we drove by two boy hitchhikers. I said 'There's two that'll
be sucking cock in about 20 minutes.'

He asked me how I could be so vulgar. I said I didn't know.

He grabbed my leg above the knee. I thought he was going to
torture/tickle, but it was a little massage that felt good and I said
so. He said 'I know. It's supposed to feel good.'
and almost crashed head on into a logging truck. I've never seen
such driving."

Lolita Spies a Satellite
At the diner where Lo consumes an unadorned burger
(HH pays the check) something across the street catches
Lo's eye (dark suit, black fedora, cardboard suitcase)
A hitchhiker clowns for no-one, doing tricks, flicks a wrist

glint in the sun
(he's got something sharp)
a butterfly knife

the shiny thing
disappears into cloth
almost as quick
as her
beady-keen eye.

Under the Sign of the Sleepwalking Bear
Her inner child died giving birth to a hellcat.
Tough little mama.
Without and never to be one
she was a tough little mama to herself.
Gold mine heart, stillborn girl
wrapped up in a motel blanket
rocking herself to sleep.
tears on your pillow
solace runs out when the quarter does
tears on your pill-
rocking.
Rock around the clock.

dream away the darkness on your
pink daisy sheets

daisies stink
snow white is found mutilated

The Couch Gathers up its Prey

Divan
Sofa
Chesterfield

Gone to die in Grey Star.

The Girl Who Trod on a Loaf

Inger
Fairy tale girl
descending into marshland
no more rainbows
no new shoes, no magic kingdom
nothing
sand in your veins
flies without wings
around your eyes
stone
immobile
a monument to conceit
burning tears –
my girl

            [She steps onto the bread]

Manna to the Gutter, 1975

Last night we got served at a bar. Justine found this cool butterfly
knife on her chair when we sat down. We drank Singapore Slings
with these creepy guys and sang the Oscar Meyer song.

We got a ride from a guy who bought us a loaf of bread and some
baloney. We made sandwiches in an abandoned tourist kiosk
outside Radium. Later we felt stupid carrying that loaf
so Justine chucked it into the ditch, where it lay near a culvert,
and was quickly covered with globs of spring snow.

Bessu Sennin: Lost Girl Satellite #2

Bodhisattva. Appears as an old man in a brown robe carrying a
staff, but may have other guises. He descends to hellish realms to
offer assistance – to save. A Good-ride Fairy. A playful saint.
A clown.

Some girls get saved. Some do. A ride that's kind, that gives
good advice, or a kindred spirit in a hostel.
The flip side of "there but for the grace of God."
A book abandoned on a bed
On the Road. The way of Zen
A signpost.

He's got something pointy in his hand.

[The diamond sutra]

Justine 2: It was her last night

Lipstick Comes Last
She puts on her good coat.
She gets into the car.
She doesn't know it's her last night on earth.

she's with him now
she's very brave.
she doesn't cry out...
anyway I like to think of her as brave
she always had more guts than I did
he carries her over the threshold
above the door is written   *birds of prey*

down to the basement of the dream home

he's laying out his instruments. he's taking his time
cut sections of telephone cord are lying on the ground
like errant sperm

he places them back on the table with his other tools
things to open the body
to determine its meaning

BRIGHT WHITE LIGHT
Johnny's got the girl

wholesome/some hole
her name is written with his forever
like a marriage license
his is the name they remember

the victims remembered have
sky blue grad photos on the cover of the Sun
happy smiles, Toni home perms
Revlon *Silverfrost Pink* lipstick
taken from schoolyards or church parking lots
honour roll virgins who didn't deserve to die

there'll be no reward for you
a whore is a murder waiting to happen

Anything is Possible in Plain View
There was no moon.
Black on black.

his hand is light on the back of my neck
as he walks me into the weeds
his voice like twigs
breaking
there's no passer-by he says
we're invisible
with the vagrants
in a city of panhandlers
and missing children

he pushed me ahead
I could hear thousand of insects
creatures

he pushed me ahead in the weeds there was no moon
I was walking ahead, I didn't look back
I wasn't sure how close behind he was
sometimes I could hear him breathe
I said, you're gonna kill me aren't you?

he said
I only kill to serve

he carries me somewhere
a basement
I'm lying face down
I can feel the twine cutting into my wrist
through the tears and blood I can see
clumps of hair on the carpet

                                        he pulls me upright

a picture of another woman on his wall
my knees…..
red juice running down my leg

                                    he's got something sharp

She was my friend. She was the wildest thing I knew.
Her real name was Mary. She was my friend.
I'm with her the day we lay down in the road and there was nobody
but us and the mountain goats.

I knew her.

Cold on the Shoulder

When I was in grade six, every month or so the whole family would get in the car for a Sunday drive in the country. We'd take Highway 2 South out of Calgary – through Midnapore, then a small town with a couple of tiny white churches and one large, brick, Gothic-looking structure called "Father Lacombe Home". Invariably, as we drove by, my Dad would glare at me and say, "If you're not careful that's where you'll end up. The home for wayward girls." It was one in a series of silent, uncomfortable rides.

At the time I wasn't quite sure what wayward meant. It's funny to me now that I didn't think "pregnancy". What I thought of as "wayward" was more serious than unwed motherhood. It was a character flaw, rather than a merely inconvenient situation. A permanent position of outsider-ness. A state of dis/grace.

A wayward girl had no back-up, no family.

She was a Ward of the Way.

Bonnie and Clyde Death Car

White Trash Haiku #15
Greasy corndog air
on the last day of Stampede
I puked by the Zipper

We are bitchin'!
We are Star Wars!
We are Stampede wrestling!

Tonight's ticket –
the Big Four versus "Crash and Burn"
You are Crash
I am Burn
we got the big splashy heave-ho
from the Big Four Building
(Bonnie and Clyde Death Car exhibit)

Rent-a-cop hauled us out
of the back seat filled with bullet holes
tore your pale blue satin shirt
(stolen from Sweet Sixteen)

Now there's no time to change if we want to ride
the Zipper
and make it
to the Corral
in time to see Queen.
Our first concert.

The carnie hard-ass
gives us a wink
our car gets an extra spin

We scream
Marc Bolan songs
as our metal cage flips us
head below feet

"You're built like a car ya got a hub cap
diamond star halo
You're dirty and sweet o yeah"

We got Star jeans
we got rhinestones
we got top hats with our names in glitter.
Crash, and: *Burn*
we got style

We are bitchin'!
We are Star Wars!
We are Stampede Wrestling!

We like swingsets
We like horses
We like attention

We love the speedway
on ladies night –
"All chicks in tube-tops
get a free pit pass!"

You're dirty sweet and you're my girl
We are bitchin'!
We are Star Wars!
We are Stampede Wrestling!

Together we're dirt track
crime spree
groupie supreme
Cherry Vanilla
Sable Starr
we are teenage wasteland
a little flame held up in the noisy dark

we mine this valley
looking for kicks
can't wait to get some
can't wait to get some

we mine the same valley lookin' for kicks
pulling fortunes out of sweaty palms.

Cold On the Shoulder

"Do I want a ride? Baby, I am a ride!"
– Dirty Babette

"Girls like you end up in dumpsters."
– random beer-parlour patron, National Hotel.

1

Hitchhiking is life writ small. My best friend Justine and I hitchhiked all over the Pacific Northwest and the Canadian prairies. We hitchhiked *within* the city just for fun and practice. Friday night was for "thumbing around" – searching for the perfect ride. If someone hopelessly square picked us up we were "just going a couple of blocks." If someone had dope – we'd ride a little further. Every time we stuck out our thumbs, we were looking for that perfect ride. We were searching for our lost people. We were lost girls.

Hitchhiking is life writ small – random choices, roads taken. Opportunities missed or disasters averted, who can say? A long line of coincidences, you don't know how far or where each ride will take you but you still remember the good ones 20 years later and the bad ones too. The ones you wonder about are the interrupted ones – the aging cowboy you refused, who wanted you to drink with him in Bellingham, the trucker on his way to LA that could have driven you straight through but he was going through Calgary and you were wanted there. How many of the good-ride-fairy gifts did you spurn?

I couldn't explain why I was always leaving, why I ran. I *could* speak to myself of the itch, I could write in balloony handwriting that I lived in a madhouse, a temple of denial, where I was the only one who shed tears or slammed doors. I'd suddenly gone from Special One to Problem Child, rage bubbling out like lava. My anger was messy, a bloody nose that wouldn't stop. It got all over people, it disgusted them. I'd fallen from grace. I felt no connection to my family. My people were elsewhere. I belonged outside the walls. I'd walk home from the ice rink, later from parties – above my head the big black empty sky, my frozen breath coming out clouds – and look up at Aurora Borealis. It was wild. The wildness stuck and, when I tried to bring it inside, it got hateful. Mean. An injured animal in a cardboard box filled with Kleenex, still strong enough to bite anyone who tried to come near.

The first time I ran away I packed a bag and left a note – the only time I did either. I was alone. I was 12 years old. I rode the city bus downtown, I still hadn't even hitchhiked yet. All the way downtown I thought about Jim Croce. I didn't even really like him, I thought his moustache was gross, but there was a song that haunted me. Something about a girl coming upon a shack in the woods and moving in with the guy who lived there. I would be that girl, I thought. I fiddled with the handle of my red vinyl Samsonite shoulder bag – it was important to travel light, I knew. I wondered if I looked OK. My hair was still long, parted in the middle and hanging straight, freshly washed in Herbal Essence and Helena Curtis Rainwater Rinse. Who knew when I'd get a chance to wash it again. The road life would be grimy. I'd probably have to bend over a sink in a gas station, or duck under a waterfall by the highway. I carried a pill container filled with Johnson's baby shampoo. It seemed the best choice. It could double as detergent. (And would explode in my bag, destroying the new *Seventeen* and a *National Lampoon*.) I'd tied a blue bandanna around my head, *Billy Jack* style. I hoped I wouldn't stick out too bad among the street people.

There was seven hours to kill before the midnight bus to Vancouver. I didn't want to waste money on the coin-operated TV's so I just sat and read my magazines. A guy that looked like Huggy Bear from Baretta tried to talk to me. I was thrilled to see an actual pimp in the flesh, not just on TV. I'd heard about what they do, though – drug you and keep you prisoner for days until you're an addict, then they turn you out – so told him I had to go. "It's because I'm black, isn't it?" I heard him say. I ran all the way to the movie theatre on Fourth street and sat through two showings of *Uptown Saturday Night*. Finally at around 9:30 I called home. My Aunt and Uncle came to pick me up, my Dad in the backseat sobbing, too upset to drive.

One year later I got a chance to really escape. It was the mid-seventies. The tail end of the earnest hitchhiker. Justine and

I stuck out among the older kids heading for hostels, jobs or college. We weren't like the others on that long hitchhike line. No backpacks, no hiking boots, not even a hand-scrawled sign. We didn't care where we went.

Every time we stuck out our thumbs, we were looking for that perfect ride – two boys, *both* cute, fun, into Bowie, lots of pot, maybe some beer and some acid or MDA. Not creepy. The rides weren't like that. Some were good in a Mark Trail kind of way – a family of cub scouts: "Look, Pop! A white-tailed deer!" I could hardly believe people like that existed. How could they even have picked us up?

We were utterly unprepared for anything, just the clothes on our backs most of the time. Our departures were always fraught with spur-of-the-moment drama. A hitch-hike home from a pool hall would turn into a ride in a converted milk truck filled with hippies going to Medicine Hat. That's how we ended up in San Francisco. I woke up all freaked out, cat hair everywhere, rug burn on my face. Justine and I had a hushed argument in the bathroom.

"We're in big shit! What are we going to do?" I said as I tore off a piece of toilet paper.

Justine was searching through the medicine chest. She picked up the least-grotty toothbrush and ran hot water over it. "Go to California."

I flushed. Yes, of course. Promised Land.

I copied her cool. "Sure. Whatever."

Justine took out her jumbo Lip Smackers – Dr. Pepper flavour. She applied it, pressed her lips together, slammed the cap down with her palm and put it in her pocket. "Frisco. That's where Kerouac went," I thought. "We can be with our people down there."

road type #3 – the kindly trucker

He'll call you "little sisters" on the CB radio and think you don't know that means "runaway". He won't turn you in (maybe you remind him a little of his own youth, his own restlessness) but he will try to convince you to call home. He'll buy you lunch. He'll

tell you not all the rides are nice guys like him. He'll let you pull
the air horn, he'll let you take turns sleeping in the berth. He'll
make a good-natured pass at the one who remains awake. He tells
you if you were his daughter he'd beat your ass until you
smartened up.

Running away made us notorious, but coming back made us
queens of the quad. By lunchtime our first day back, we'd have a
few disciples. Skinny grade sevens with Star jeans and platform
shoes. Loner-girls with thick journals and thicker glasses.
Hitchiking was still a done thing in Trudeau's Canada. Scholastic
Magazine even had hints for hitting the road: "At a greasy spoon,
always order grilled cheese. You're less likely to get sick that way."
The advice we dispensed in the lunchroom was entirely our own.

highway con #4 – free pot
Both of you get in the front. Ask the driver if he wants to smoke
a joint. After smoking one, he will ask you to roll one from *his*
stash. Comply. Middle girl engages him in conversation, while
the girl closest to the window rolls. As she rolls, she puts several
joints worth into her foil-lined jean jacket pocket especially
prepared for this purpose. When he drops you off, roll your own
joint out of stolen pot. Repeat with next ride.

We were con-artists. Pint-sized Villons. Highwaymen. Our age
kept us safe. If someone was getting too persistent and we wanted
them to lay off, we just had to mention that magic number – 13 –
and they would stop whatever they started. Most of the time.
Lots of times we couldn't be bothered with any kind of
invocation – too drunk, too stoned, or maybe they were cute, or
maybe so what.

road type # 9 – the talent cobra
This guy drives a nice new car and asks you if you're a model or
actress. He tells you have the looks for it. He has prescription
drugs, and sometimes comes complete with an aggressive bisexual
wife. (She will get into the back with your friend while you take

the front.) He's more dangerous if alone. If he offers you powder, hedge against famine. If he offers you pills, chipmunk ("Hide them in your cheek, stupid!") for later. *Do not consume while in the car.* You can't win this one, don't even try.

highway con #5 – free hotel rooms
You're picked up by two guys, both dorks. You get them to go and get beer and then you suggest getting a motel. When you get there send both of them off to get something else: food, condoms, whatever. They will go because they will want to discuss who gets who. Then lock them out. Listen to them outside, hear them pound furiously on the door. Don't worry. They go away. You've told them your age, and they are most likely wanted.

We were the Marquis de Sade's libertines for real – the scene in *Go Ask Alice* with the sadist couple just seemed like the coolest part of the lifestyle.

Sure, crawl like dogs in our underwear. Why not?

Button, button, just keep us stoned and amused and we'll bark up any old tree you like.

And if we don't wanna fuck you we'll figure out a way of getting your dope anyway, plus a motel room, if we can. If we're at your house we'll help ourselves to old coins, your wife's pretty clothes. We can strip a master bedroom in seconds flat. We'll come out of the bathroom wearing nothing but a smile, in which we've hidden all your prescription drugs. "They wouldn't know the difference. All *they* can think about is getting in our pants."

We were hard-hearted. It's easy to say today I was searching for transcendence. Truth is we were searching for drink, drugs, cock, excitement and fucked-up times. We needed to lose, we needed to surf a volcano. We needed chaos on the outside to match the chaos on the inside. We lied all the time and didn't care about anything.

One time we got stuck just outside of Radium. We must have walked at least 20 miles. It was sunny and warm on the road. We smoked a joint and talked about Patti Smith.

"I'm gonna meet her." I said.

"Yeah right."

"I *am*."

"Even if you *could* find her and meet her, there's no way you'd have anything to say to her."

"Would too!" I grabbed the joint away from her.

On a bluff about 20 feet away the snow was melting making little frozen waterfalls. The road curved around the side of a cut through a mountain. No cars in sight. *It doesn't matter if you walk down the middle of the road.* Justine looked at me dubiously out of the corner of her eye.

"OK, pretend I'm her."

She walked away all snobby-like. I ran to catch up with her. She froze me like a socialite and kept walking. I jumped in front of her. "Hey! *Hey...Miss Smith?* I hear you like Rimbaud! I like Rimbaud too! I even know some off by heart –

It is she, the little girl
dead behind the rose bushes –"

Justine looked surprised and grinned. "OK, I guess she would want to meet you."

We kept walking and walking, finally just lying in the middle of the highway. The black attracts warmth. The tarmac felt so good on our backs, the sun on our faces.

"Justine. Justine! Check it out!"

Two mountain goats were watching us from up on the plateau. There was no-one around for miles.

"Justine, what time do you think it is?"

"I dunno. Oh shit, here comes a car."

We scrambled off the road just as a schoolbus passed us. Something flew out the window.

"Did that kid just chuck a sandwich at us?"

I was cold. We only had minimum clothing – we were dressed for a Chinook a week ago when we took off on the spur of the moment. All we'd added to our layers along the way were a couple of stolen jackets. "What are we gonna do? We've been out here forever! It's getting fucking *cold*."

"Why do you always ask me what to do? As if I know any

more than you do? "

We kept walking. It was really getting cold. Finally we found a trailer on a farm.

"You talk." I hissed as I knocked. To me it was a fair exchange.

"No, YOU" – Justine's voice caught as the door opened.

A double-wide woman filled the doorway. "You girls got a problem?"

Farmers are like artists. They live in worry and isolation. Themselves and the land. Imagine the situation. He is in a trailer, his wife gone to fat, her brownies the antidote to her loneliness which increases continuously, like her ass, over the years. When she went into the kitchen to get us some food, Justine and I avoided each other's eyes. We knew what we'd say later.

"The biggest ass I've ever seen. *Ever.* "

We raided the change jar. It's the only time we felt bad for anything we did. Even now I feel bad. They were good, kind people. We didn't run into too many of those.

We are lost girls, but we're also prairie girls. We know the thrill-chill of an autumn indigo morning, even if seeing it from the wrong end, slouching home in the acid dawn.

When our ancestors came West the train dropped them off, and there they stood, bundles in hand, surveying land not yet defined, days not yet lived. An infinite number of possibilities.

These plains fuel us and oppress us. Is it any wonder we fetishize that which takes us away? Lie down in the middle of the road. Go ahead, mix it up with hot tar. Put your ear to the ground. The rumbling speaks of dreams, of running West till the water stops you, till there no place to go but crazy. A highway is a fossil, it contains the yearning of those who drive over it, looking for their lives. Turn over. *It's OK, there's no cars for miles.* Feel the pavement against your cheek, and remember, face down on the ground there's no place left to fall.

The best times Justine and I had were waiting for rides. Even though it seemed like a drag, we had each other. We'd sit on the shoulder or lie in the middle of the road, we'd skip the road altogether and bound through the ditch, skirting barbed wire and running crazy in the mustard-coloured fields. We could talk about anything we wanted, didn't have to dumb it down for some asshole ride. The men were always in our faces. How many times did we laugh at their book and record collections when they left the room?

Where were our people? Where was our tribe of twisted fire? We searched for clues. We deciphered, experimented. We read *Creem* magazine religiously, scouring Lester Bangs for references to our lost tribe.

Lenny Bruce. Jack Kerouac. Lou Reed. Patti Smith.

We could have bullshitted our way in anywhere, only, in 1975, anywhere was somehow so low-grade. We saw with TV eyes raised on *Baretta* and *Dawn: Portrait of a Teenage Runaway*. Beat downtown locales. Street people, the grit.

We thought we would find our people. We didn't. We had each other.

We had matching drawstring blue jeans we stole from a Saan store in Nanaimo, Justine slapping me in the change room because I was too chicken to wrap them under my shirt. She took both and I pocketed two muslin peasant tops. We wore them out to the bar that night and met two guys who bought us Tequila Sunrises and a hotel room. We did the bump in front of the nailed-on mirror in our matching outfits, and sent them out for pizza. Last thing I heard was Justine telling them to fuck off through the chain while I puked red. In the morning we had continental breakfast.

There was no excuse to stop. Not blood, not tears, not anything anyone could throw could drive a wedge between us.

We could handle most guys, we thought, till we met our first Talent Cobra. Talent Cobras got the goods but don't try to put one over. "You can't con a con" is the Talent Cobra motto. Talent Cobra's not like those other guys. *Not* in a good way. He drives casually while you girls (one in front, one in back) down the pills. He keeps up an oblivious British banter that sounds like Bond through a wind tunnel. Soon one of you is throwing up out the window.

"I'm not going to hurt you. I promise." When a ride says that you better be ready to bail. This is a private tutorial in the use and abuse of power. There're so many places to land on the sliding sadist scale. Some men will stop at nothing, others will be scared off by a look, a scream.

bad ride # 32 – a timid cobra

He's scared to finish what he started so he drops you off between a McDonald's and a Wendy's while you hold your friend's head. Too disoriented to give a flipping finger to his taillights. Inhaling his dust. Eating his exhaust. She passes out. You roll her onto her side so she won't die. You survey your situation. You can't move her. You're hallucinating behind a dumpster, no place to stay tonight. The sky's still there. *Hi big sky.*

Next night we met a guy, pretty slick for a small town, he got us a motel room with double-double beds. We were tired, he was cute. What the hell. Two double beds. One lost girl in each. Back and forth the would-be pimp beats a path in red shag. Matching drawstring jeans lie at the foot of each bed. I have to go to the bathroom in the middle of the night but I don't want to because I'm naked from the waist down. Justine is my best friend. Her voice comes floating, sex-sated, a late night drawl. She wants me to go outside. She says they want to be alone. I'm furious and go to the all-night coffee shop. I stay there all night and when I come back in the morning she's gone. I decide to hitchhike East alone. I think I saw her going the other way with the motel guy and some other big guy but I'm not sure. Next time I saw her was in Chinatown, in Vancouver, years after we were best friends. She was wearing a yellow blouse that made her look frail. *She was never frail.*

Justine said, "It's embarrassing to run into you like this, with me workin'." I had to go. She had to make money. Her mother had died in a hotel fire. It was 1979 and it was the last time I hitchhiked. My good-ride fairies had quit me and every single ride after that was a weirdo.

Hitchhiking is life writ small.

2

The winter I was five it never got above 40 below. Dads still had to go to work but schools were closed for two weeks. After my Dad left for the office my Mom would go back to bed and I'd crawl in with her. We'd eat Cap'n Crunch and she'd tell me about her old beaux. Before she met my Dad she went out with a guy, a twin, only he wasn't really a twin. His Mom was the eldest daughter, she'd got pregnant at 14, the same time as her mother, and both boys were raised as brothers. My mother was seeing the good boy (the son), but he went out of town and my Mom started seeing the bad one (the nephew). He was two months older than the good son but scrawny and his own grandmother/mother said he must've been bit by a black snake the day he was born. He had a handsome face and smelled like a carnival. "His kisses tasted like cotton candy, sweet and dangerous," my Mom said. She reached out for her cigarettes. I handed them to her with the red ceramic ashtray. She scooted up in bed and grabbed the other pillow. She put it behind her head, lit her smoke and shielded her eyes. I adjusted the curtains and put the empty bowls on the floor so I could curl up beside her.

"So I was running with the bad son and we'd drive and drive till we were a few towns over and we'd go into the ladies and escorts entrance at the beer parlour and I'd would get up with the band and sing."

After the boyfriend story came my favorite part. Still lying in bed, she'd sing me every Hank Williams song ever written. She told me I was robbed of a Texan girlhood because she was too chicken to run. The way she told it, the man she adored came for us all the way from Houston to Calgary in a red sports car. It was Spring, I was 18 months old and we drove out to Bragg Creek and had a picnic in the pussy-willows. That's when he asked her to come stateside. My Mom had to stop at home to get her things, and there she ran into her Mom and lost her nerve. She didn't want to be disowned. She stayed. She had to. She'd grown up under the shadow of disownment – her Mother, my Nana, was disowned. My Mother told my Nana's tale breathlessly – romance on the range, elopement on the prairie, always with the cautionary addendum about what happens when you give in fully to your wildest urges. My Nana had followed her heart's desire, and where had it left her? With a baby coming every nine months, stranded at seventeen with three babies and a husband who was never home. (It was whispered he was a bootlegger.) So my Mom was too chicken to run. She stayed. It was 15 years before I'd see Texas.

I was third generation restless. What I know about my Nana's brief youth I know through my Mom.

My Nana was as close to being a spoiled rich girl as you could be in depression-era Saskatchewan. She was an only child and drove her own Packard. She had the best wardrobe in town. When she was sixteen she ran away with a stray man from outside – he'd come through on a paving crew, turning the dirt roads into tarmac. It was as if she was waiting for him to pave the way out. She ran. Her Mother never spoke to her again.

I was robbed of a Texan girlhood but I still had the Big Sky. On Saturdays my Dad took us to see spaghetti westerns. *Trinity is Still my Name. Heller in Pink Tights.* The dance-hall girls, with their green stockings and horse-drawn caravans, were my idols. When we left the theater the real big sky was waiting. It was like living in a Western every day. In the movies, on the boardwalk streets, the good townswomen pulled their skirts to the side as they passed by the dance-hall girls. How could those townswomen walk a straight line? How could they not put a foot wrong? How could they manage to draw boundaries amongst all that space, all that wildness?

When my Mom talked about her beaux it was the dance-hall girls I pictured. I saw my Mother in a black and green outfit, fishnet tights and feathers in her hair, like a Klondike Days costume. When she talked about the places her boyfriends took her, it was a cowboy saloon that came to mind, my Mom standing in the corner on a tiny stage, singing a big ol' song.

"I'd get up on stage and sing 'Your Cheatin' Heart', and I'd dance barefoot on his cowboy boots. And on the way home he'd get the car going way over sixty and turn out the headlights, and we'd both scream as loud as we could all the way home because it felt so good."

Those winter mornings. She'd always finish her stories with a tune – "Your Cheatin' Heart." I'd lie down and watch the dust swirl in the sunbeam. It was a feeling. Later I'd feel the same way about kicking in plate glass windows.

Then it would be time to bring her water to take her pill. I'd fluff her pillow and –

"Close the door, puppy" – leave her sleeping.

Sleeping thick woolly sleep under piles of blankets. Dead Wood winter. Dreaming of meadows and casting 40-foot shadows on mountains.

I don't mean to imply that my mother never ran. She tried escape too, the summer she was nine. She'd fallen and broken her arm. Her Mom had to bend it back and forth every night.

"Back and forth every night. *Every night*. Back and forth till I could have spit on the floor. So I wouldn't have a crooked arm." She dragged on her cigarette. "One night I couldn't stand it any longer and I packed a suitcase. I marched right out, past my Mother standing at the sink. Out the back door, past the Conky's house, past the grain elevator. Over to the railroad tracks. I was going to hide in the grain car once it was filled and ride as far as it went. I lay down on the tracks, put my head on the steel. It was still warm. I fell asleep and dreamed perfect daylight. When I woke up there was your Nana, holding out my sweater and a mug of warm milk."

I think my Mother knew the Lost Girl feeling. Walking out into the dark by yourself, your house glowing warm behind you and the cold unknown ahead, there's a pull home has, yes, but you've broken through a membrane and now it's just you and the stars.

Family vacations were the era of the earnest hitchhiker. We'd beg our Dad to pick one up – all those 60's young people holding up cardboard signs. *Vancouver Island. Kamloops.* He would never give anyone a ride; sign or not, he'd always say, "They want to go farther than we can take them."

Sex Tangles

What did I think the first time I saw you?
That I could really fuck you up
like a terrorist.
Cruel, cold, completely crazy
Blowing up your bank line-up.
C'mon. Slip into my squalour.
I could fuck you up. Make you lose.
Malevolent manifestoes dancing around the back of my head.
The back of my head you held and screamed when I gave you
the best blow-job you'd ever had.
I fucked you up.
You weren't yourself.
You were a wild thing from outside.
You orbited in a whole other galaxy
an alien god
twisting my hair into tangles at the back of my neck.

"tonight we sleep in separate ditches"

I crawled into the ditch.
I was looking for a lost comb
and I came upon
a rag
a bone
a hank of hair
                    artifacts of a struggle

Good thing I stopped hitchhiking in the seventies.
While the unwanted click of an automatic door lock was not
unknown to me
neither did I have to fight
the futile fight.
Not in a car, anyway.
The last time I hitchhiked was 1979, out of necessity.
I'd long since discarded the yearning for that
Jack Kerouac Experience.

The last time I hitchhiked, every single ride was a weirdo.
It's amazing how many different ways there are to be a weirdo –
jovial frat boys looking for a gang-bang
propositioning salesmen with baby seats in the back of their
Cutlass Supreme
sad, desperate hand-holders in Porsches extending
tentative tentacles across the gear shift.

I'm pretty sure it was Clifford Olsen took me
for french fries and gravy.
We stopped somewhere on the Trans-Canada –
he offered me lunch.
I stuck to the rules (order the cheapest thing on the menu)
he starts talking this weird shit –
cattle mutilations, effects of in-breeding,
fathers fucking daughters, Armageddon –
then he stops. He says
"What's the matter, is all of this sounding a little too familiar?"
I just looked out the window and finished those fries.
I told him I have friends around here, I don't need to go any
further...

As he was paying the check I noticed a hand-made poster taped
to the wall.
A missing girl.
He saw me looking at it.
He smiled.
Said good-bye to the waitress by name.

I'm often thinking of men who kill.
Are they evolutionary throwbacks to Australopithicus?
Or are they products of a neo-barbarian future where guys say
Yeah. She's *damn* cute. I'd bash her head in with a rock.

White Trash Haiku #714

Inside the warm car
windshield wipers hypnotize
grey day, green trees – *hushhhhhh*.

Ali Riley was born in Calgary, where she was the lead singer/songwriter of Sacred Heart of Elvis, a seminal 80's psycho-country band. In Toronto she acted in various theatre productions (*The Lorca Play*, *When There Was No Money Left in The World*, *Das Rheingold*), along the way aquiring skills such as Flamenco dance and walking through broken glass whilst chewing on a pig's heart. Her produced plays include *dog dream*, *Philosophy in the Bedroom*, *Hole in My Heart the Size of My Heart*, and *Schadenfreude Funhaus*. In 1999 she moved to a cabin in Winlaw, BC. and lived off the grid. She currently lives on a farm between Nanton and Vulcan, Alberta.